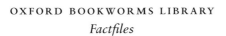

OXFORD BOOKWORMS LIBRARY

Factfiles

The Life and Diaries of Anne Frank

RACHEL BLADON

Stage 3 (1000 headwords)

Series Editor: Rachel Bladon
Founder Factfiles Editor: Christine Lindop

OXFORD
UNIVERSITY PRESS

Great Clarendon Street, Oxford, OX2 6DP, United Kingdom

Oxford University Press is a department of the University of Oxford.
It furthers the University's objective of excellence in research, scholarship,
and education by publishing worldwide. Oxford is a registered trade
mark of Oxford University Press in the UK and in certain other countries

ISBN: 978 0 19 402285 9

A complete recording of this Bookworms edition of
The Life and Diaries of Anne Frank is available.

Printed in China

Word count (main text): 12,592

For more information on the Oxford Bookworms Library,
visit www.oup.com/elt/gradedreaders

ACKNOWLEDGEMENTS

Cover Image: A picture of Anne Frank from 1941 released by the Anne Frank
Fonds in Frankfurt Main, Germany/dpa picture alliance Archive/Alamy.

Illustrations by: Peter Bull p.2 (map).

The publisher would like to thank the following for permission to reproduce photographs:
Alamy Images pp.6 (Earl Young/Art Directors & TRIP), 7 (Chronicle), 21 (dpa
picture alliance), 50 (Auschwitz tattoo/ITAR-TASS Photo Agency), 52 (liberation
of Bergen Belsen/War Archive, Memorial to Anne and Margot Frank/Ronals
Wilfred Jansen), 57 (Endless Travel), 74 (Paul Fearn); Anne Frank House,
Amsterdam pp.0 (large Anne portrait/small inset portrait), 1 (closed diary), 3, 4,
11, 12 (Oma Rosa Hollander), 14, 17, 22, 23 (Anne at Lyceum), 30 (Illustration by
Chantal van Wessel and Frederik Ruys www.vizualism.com © 2010, 2012 Anne
Frank Stichting, Amsterdam), 31, 35; Dutch Resistance Museum, Amsterdam
p.28; Getty Images pp.0 (diary page/Anne and Margot on beach/Anne Frank
Fonds Basel), 9 (Anne Frank Fonds Basel), 10 (Anne Frank Fonds Basel), 12 (Oma
Alice Frank/Anne Frank Fonds Basel), 13 (Anne Frank Fonds Basel), 15 (Hulton
Archive/Stringer), 18-19 (Three Lions/Stringer), 20 (exterior 263 Prinsengracht/
Anne Frank Fonds Basel, typewriter/Martyn Goddard/Corbis Documentary),
33 (CBS Photo Archive), 37 (Anne Frank Fonds Basel), 40 (Albert De Jong/AFP),
41 (US Army Forces/FPG), 42 (Gordon Coster/The LIFE Picture Collection),
45 (Anne Frank Fonds Basel), 47 (Ullstein Bild), 49 (Galerie Bilderwelt), 50 (bunks
at Auschwitz/Galerie Bilderwelt, prisoners in queue/Ullstein bild), 55 (Kyodo
News), 59 (Ullstein bild); Mary Evans Picture Library p.16 (Interfoto); NIOD/
Beeldbank WO2, Amsterdam p.24; Rex/Shutterstock pp.48 (Granger), 54 (Sipa
Press); Shutterstock p.23 (projector/Victor Baril).

Activities written by: Nicole Irving.

CONTENTS

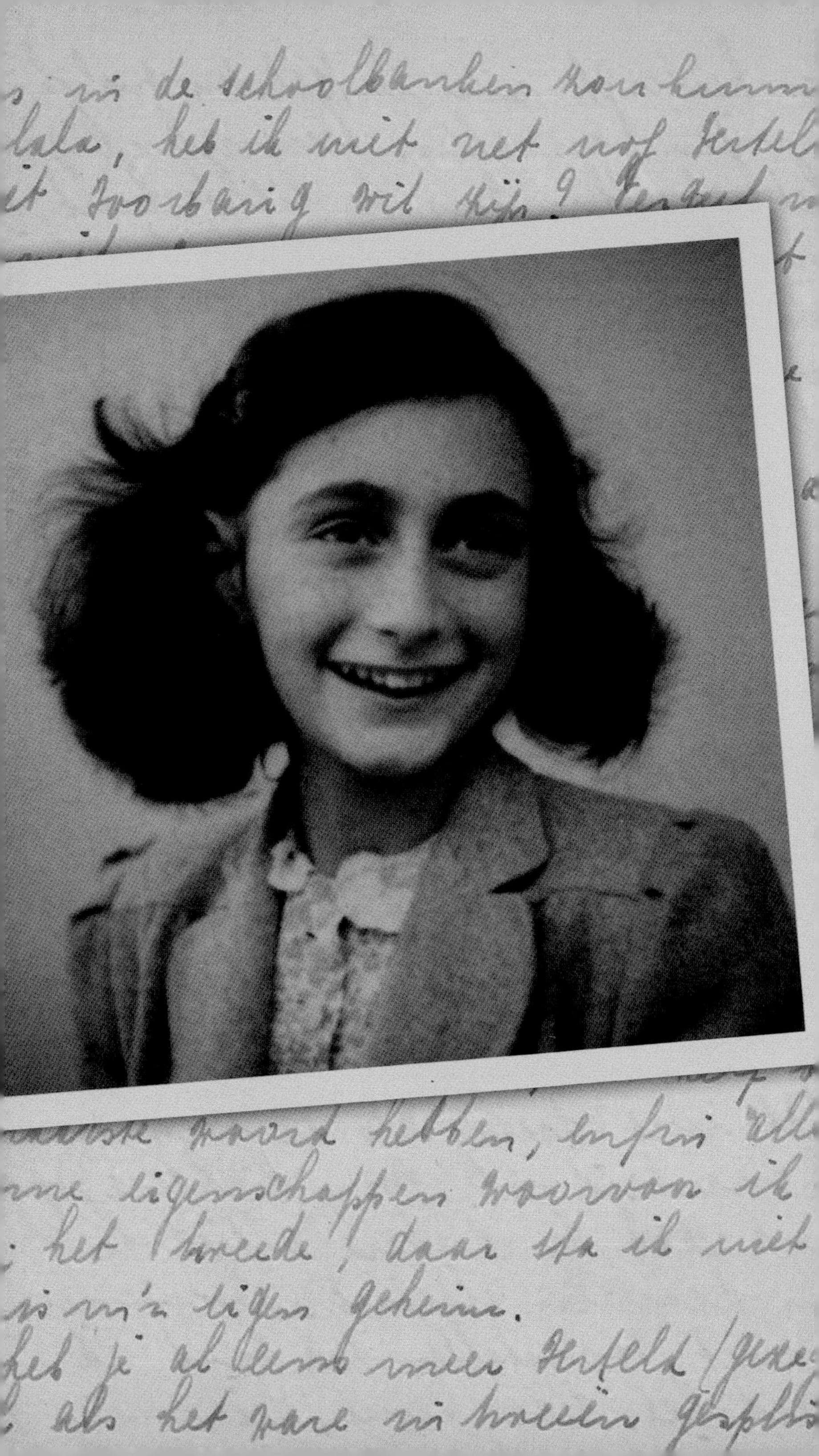

1   A birthday present

It is June 1942, and Europe is at war. In Amsterdam, in the Netherlands, a young girl runs excitedly into the sitting room of her family's large apartment early one morning. She is not thinking about the world's problems today: it is her thirteenth birthday, and as her parents watch, she looks happily at the presents that they have arranged on the table for her.

There are books and flowers, a game, some money, sweets, and a cake. But among these, the girl finds the present that she wanted most of all, and takes it in her hands. It is a square notebook with a red, white, and green cover and a little metal lock. She has wanted the notebook since she saw it in a shop window with her father a few days earlier. It will be her diary.

Anne Frank's diary

That girl, enjoying her birthday and her first day as a teenager, was called Anne Frank. Only a few weeks later, her life changed in the most extraordinary – and terrible – way. And because of the things that happened to her over the next three years, and what she wrote about them in her diaries, the story of Anne Frank is now famous around the world.

Europe, 1939

2 Early years: Frankfurt, 1929–1933

Anne Frank was born on 12ᵗʰ June 1929 in the city of Frankfurt in Germany. From the start, she was very different from her sister Margot. Margot, who was three years older, had been a quiet and easy baby, but little Anne did not like to sleep much during the day, and cried all night.

As she grew into a small child, Anne was fun and full of life, but no one could tell her what to do or what not to do. She was still the opposite of her sister Margot, who was quiet and polite and, it seemed, never did anything wrong.

The girls' parents, Otto and Edith Frank, made a lot of time for their children. Otto Frank was an unusual father: in the 1920s and 1930s, most men did not spend a lot of time with their children, but although Otto Frank's job kept him very busy, he loved playing with Anne and her sister Margot, and he read to them as much as he could.

Margot and Anne, 1933

Otto and Edith Frank were educated people who came from large and successful families. Otto Frank's family had lived in Frankfurt for hundreds of years, and there was a family business and bank in the city. By 1929, Otto was working for the family business, but he had had jobs with other companies before, in different German cities, and in New York and Amsterdam.

Anne and Margot's mother Edith came from Aachen, in the west of Germany, and when the girls were little, their parents often took them there to visit their grandmother (Edith's mother, who they called 'Oma Hollander') and two uncles (Edith's brothers). Edith's father was dead, but in his lifetime, he had been important among the Jewish people in Aachen, and when Edith was younger, she had gone most weeks to the synagogue there with her family. Otto was Jewish, too, but being Jewish was not so important to him; and Otto and Edith celebrated non-Jewish festivals, like Christmas, with their children, as well as Jewish ones.

Otto Frank with Margot and Anne

Edith Frank

Just a few months after Anne was born in 1929, the world economy crashed. Prices fell, companies stopped buying and selling things, and millions of people lost their jobs. Times were very hard for many in Germany, and for the Frank family bank and business, too. In 1931, Otto and Edith had to move with their children from the apartment where they had lived for four years to a smaller, less expensive one.

Anne was nearly two years old by that time. She spent her days playing happily with her sister and the neighbours' children. But while her parents watched them play, they knew that a dark storm was coming.

A new political party – Adolf Hitler's Nazi party – was becoming more and more important in Germany. The Nazis promised the people of Germany a better future. After the First World War, which had ended more than ten years earlier, in 1918, Germany had lost a lot of land. The Nazis promised to win back this land, and to make jobs for people.

Hitler knew what the German people wanted to hear. *It was people like the Jews*, Hitler told them, *who had lost the First World War for 'true' Germans, and who had taken their jobs and their money. Now,* Hitler promised, *the Nazis would make the 'true people' of Germany strong once more.*

Hitler was a clever speaker, and when he talked, people listened to him and believed him. Only 3% of German voters had chosen the Nazi party in 1928, but in July 1932, 37% voted for them.

For Otto and Edith Frank, these were strange and frightening times. Otto had fought for Germany in the First World War, and in many ways, being German was more important to him than being Jewish. He loved his country, and he hoped that people would soon understand how dangerous Hitler and the Nazis really were.

Adolf Hitler, 1928

By 1932, groups of Nazi soldiers called 'storm troopers' had begun to appear on the streets of Frankfurt. They shouted terrible songs about Jewish blood falling from knives. Otto and Edith heard their shouts, and knew that they had to leave their home city. But where would they go? And how would they find work for Otto, and be able to live?

In January 1933, Hitler became Chancellor of Germany – the most important person in the country. And with the help of his storm troopers, who frightened everyone, he was able to take control of the government, and stop any non-Nazi political parties who did not agree with his ideas.

The Nazis putting a poster on a Jewish shop, 1933

Hitler began to make life difficult for Jewish people in Germany. On 1st April 1933, the Nazis told people to stop using Jewish shops and businesses, and even Jewish doctors and dentists. Schools had to send Jewish teachers away, too. In Frankfurt and other German cities, many Jewish businesses soon had no money and had to close. Otto and Edith also began to hear stories of attacks on Jewish people.

In March 1933, Otto and Edith left their apartment and moved with their two young daughters back to the Frank family home, where Otto had lived as a child. They had decided to leave Germany, and they needed to be ready to go quickly.

Otto had heard about a job in the Netherlands. His sister's husband worked for a company called Opekta that made products for jam-making, and the company was looking for a manager for the business in Amsterdam. This seemed like just the right job for Otto. He had worked in Amsterdam ten years before, so he knew the city and the Dutch language. And because many Jewish people already lived in Amsterdam, he hoped that his family would be safe there.

3   Amsterdam, 1933–1939

In summer 1933, Otto moved to Amsterdam to begin his new job with Opekta. Edith took Anne and Margot to Aachen to stay with her mother, Oma Hollander, and her brothers, Julius and Walter. From there, she travelled to Amsterdam several times to find a home for the family and get it ready for her daughters.

Soon after Otto left Frankfurt, his mother left the Frank family home, too, and moved to Basel in Switzerland. 'Omi Frank', as Anne and Margot called her, was the last one of her close family to leave Germany. Like Otto, her other sons and her daughter all now lived in different countries around Europe.

Edith and Otto Frank found an apartment for their family in Merwedeplein, a new part of Amsterdam in the south of the city. They moved there in December 1933, and soon after, Julius and Walter brought Margot to Amsterdam from Aachen, while Anne stayed with Oma Hollander. Margot had to start at her new Dutch school in January, so Otto and Edith wanted to help her with that before Anne arrived.

Anne was brought to Amsterdam two months later, in February 1934, and her arrival was a surprise for Margot. When Margot came into the sitting room on the morning of her eighth birthday, Anne was sitting on the table with her other presents!

Anne was nearly five years old by then. She was a happy little girl, who was full of ideas. She knew what she wanted, too, so she was sometimes difficult – but she liked to have fun. She did not go to school at first when she arrived in Amsterdam, so while Margot was at school, she was bored. She missed her friends in Frankfurt and the family in Aachen, so Edith sent her back to Aachen several times to visit her grandmother and her uncles, who she loved dearly.

But in April, Anne began at a kindergarten – a school for very young children – just a short walk from her home. Many German Jewish families, escaping from the Nazis, had come to live in that part of Amsterdam, and Anne soon became good friends with two girls called Hanneli Goslar and Susanne Ledermann. Like her, they had both come from Germany. People called the three girls Hanne, Sanne, and Anne – and they were always together.

Anne (right) with her friend Susanne

Margot

Anne

Merwedeplein, 1935

The buildings in Merwedeplein, where Anne and Hanneli both lived, stood around a square, and after school, the children all went out there to play games and run around together.

For Anne and Margot, who both had new friends, and who quickly began to learn Dutch, life in Amsterdam was happy and fun. Their friends loved visiting their home. Mrs Frank liked to put special food on the table for her daughters' friends – and everybody loved Mr Frank, who always seemed cheerful. Anne and Margot and their friends could talk and laugh about anything with him, and he always had ideas for games, or stories to tell. Anne and Margot thought that he was wonderful, and they had a special name for him: 'Pim'.

Unlike her daughters, Edith was finding her new life hard. The Franks' apartment in Amsterdam was much smaller than the ones where they had lived in Frankfurt, and Edith had no one to help her with housework now. She missed Germany, and she found the Dutch language difficult – and she worried about her family at home in Aachen, too.

She was not alone: there were many other German mothers in Amsterdam who were finding life hard, and talking to them helped Edith. Hanneli's parents soon became good friends with the Franks, and on Friday evenings, the Frank family often went to the Goslars' home for the beginning of the Sabbath, the most important time of the week for Jewish people.

By March 1935, Anne was nearly six years old, and ready to move from kindergarten into 'real school'. She did not go to the school where Margot was a student. Instead, Anne stayed at the school where she was already, which had classes for older students, too. It was a new school, with modern ideas, and students could choose how they wanted to spend their day. Anne was always asking questions, and loved being with people and doing different things – so it suited her well. Anne was reading a lot by this time, after a slow start, and she had started to enjoy writing stories, too. But she was not as hard-working as her sister Margot.

Anne's school, 1935

As a young girl, Anne was often ill, and she sometimes had to stay away from school for several weeks. She had to miss a lot of sports lessons at school, too, because she had problems with her legs, and her shoulder dislocated very easily – her arm often pulled out of it. But for Anne, this was not always a bad thing. It looked very funny when it happened, so she often dislocated it herself just to make her friends laugh.

There were many happy times in Merwedeplein. Anne and Margot's grandmother, Oma Hollander, and their uncles, Julius and Walter, often came to stay, and there were visits from other people in the Hollander and Frank families, too.

In 1935 and 1936, Anne went to Switzerland to visit her other grandmother, Omi Frank (Otto's mother), and stayed with her in a beautiful house which belonged to one of Otto's cousins. On her visits to Omi Frank, Anne also enjoyed spending time with her cousin Bernd. He was four years older than her, but they loved playing together, and they liked to put on their grandmother's clothes and do short theatre plays for the adults.

Oma Hollander   Omi Frank

There were still family holidays and days out for the Franks at this time, too. From summer 1934, they often went to Zandvoort am Zee, a town by the sea near Amsterdam. In summer 1937, Anne and Margot went with their parents to the sea at Middelkerke in Belgium; and in March 1938, they went by boat around the Dutch lakes.

Anne and Margot at the beach, 1935

Because Otto Frank was always cheerful, Anne probably did not know that behind his kind smiles, he had many troubles during these years. The Opekta business did not do well at first, and he spent a lot of time travelling and working, but made only a little money. In 1938, together with another businessman, Johannes Kleiman, who Otto had known and worked with for many years, he opened a new company called Pectacon, which sold spices and other products for cooking. Otto and Kleiman knew nothing about spices, but they soon found someone who did: Hermann van Pels. Like Otto, van Pels and his family were Jewish, and they had come to Amsterdam from Germany to escape Hitler's Nazis. After van Pels joined Pectacon, he and his wife Auguste and their son Peter soon began to visit the Frank family home as friends.

Otto and Edith Frank liked to invite friends to their home for coffee on a Saturday afternoon. Many of those who came were Jewish people who had escaped from Germany; but there were Dutch friends, too. Miep Santrouschitz, Otto's secretary, had quickly become a good friend of the family, and she and her boyfriend Jan Gies often came to the Franks' house. Another Dutch visitor for those Saturday afternoon coffees was Bep Voskuijl, a tall, quiet, and kind young woman who also worked for Otto.

Opekta/Pectacon workers
Left to right: Miep Santrouschitz, Johannes Kleiman,
Otto Frank, Victor Kugler, Bep Voskuijl

The Franks did not have a lot of money at that time, but they knew that they were luckier than many, and Edith always made good food for their friends when they came to the apartment. On those Saturday afternoons, they talked a lot about what the Nazis were doing in Germany. They all knew from their friends that life in Germany was getting harder and harder for Jewish people. Everyone who had friends or family or the chance of a job in another country was leaving.

Edith and Otto were becoming more and more worried about Edith's mother and brothers, who still lived in Aachen. And on 9th November 1938, Edith and Otto's fears became very real. That night, which was later called 'Kristallnacht', Nazi storm troopers ran through the streets of Germany's towns and cities, destroying synagogues and Jewish homes and businesses. 236 people were murdered on Kristallnacht, and in the days after, thirty thousand Jewish men were arrested and taken to concentration camps. These were places like prisons that the Nazis had built from 1933, where they sent Jews and their other 'enemies'. The camps were dirty, cold, and uncomfortable, and full of disease and illness. Prisoners there had to do very hard work, and were punished terribly for the smallest things.

A burning synagogue Kristallnacht, 9th November 1938

Sachsenhausen concentration camp

Julius and Walter Hollander – Anne and Margot's uncles – were among the men who were taken to concentration camps in November 1938. Because Julius had fought for Germany in the First World War, he was not kept as a prisoner for long, but Walter was taken to the Sachsenhausen concentration camp near Berlin, and was then told to leave the country.

Julius knew that he and his mother, Oma Hollander, needed to leave Germany, too. But because so many Jewish people were leaving Germany by that time, other countries were beginning to close their doors: they did not want to let too many people move in. Oma Hollander could go and live in Amsterdam, she was told, but Julius and Walter could not. So the two brothers decided to move to the US, where one of their cousins lived. Julius was able to go at once, but Walter, who was still in a Nazi camp, had to follow later.

Before Julius left Germany in March 1939, the Hollander family business that he had directed with his brother was closed by the Nazis. The family lost nearly everything that they had owned. Julius brought Oma Hollander, deeply distressed, to live with Edith, Otto, Anne, and Margot in Amsterdam. Then he left for the US. He was followed by Walter nine months later – and the two brothers never saw their mother again.

4 First years of war, 1939–1942

Anne loved Oma Hollander dearly, and she was happy when her grandmother came to live in Amsterdam with the Frank family. Anne was nearly ten years old by this time, and was working hard at school. She loved her teacher Hendrika Kuperus, who did plays and theatre studies with her students. Mrs Kuperus thought that Anne's ideas for plays were very good, and she liked the clever, interesting language that she used. But Anne sometimes got into trouble for talking too much. Her friends liked being with her, because she was funny and full of life, although sometimes she said what she thought a little too strongly, and was too sure of herself.

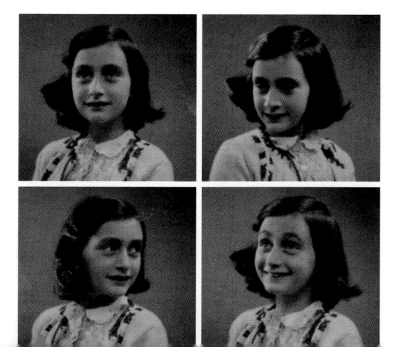

Anne's parents had tried hard to hide their worries about what was happening in Germany from her and Margot, but by early 1939, they could not keep their fears secret. Nazi soldiers had already invaded Austria and Czechoslovakia by that time, and in September 1939, they moved into Poland. France and Britain had promised to keep Poland safe, and they told Hitler to take his soldiers out of the country. But Hitler did not listen. France and Britain were now at war with Germany.

The Netherlands had been neutral in the First World War – the country had not fought on either side – so Otto Frank had hoped that his family would be safe there. But from early 1939, he and Edith became afraid that Germany would attack the Netherlands, too. And on 10th May 1940, the day they had feared came: Hitler's armies invaded the country.

There was no school for Anne or her friends that day, and as it was a Friday, they were probably excited at first to have a long weekend. But it was frightening for them, too. All day, people listened to the radio, terrified. Some people, afraid to find themselves without food, bought everything that they could from the shops. Many Jewish people tried desperately to leave the Netherlands, by car or by bicycle, but most were stopped and sent back. Some, terrified of the future, killed themselves because they were afraid to live in a Nazi country.

After a few difficult and frightening days, with fighting in other parts of the country, the Dutch government surrendered: they told Hitler that they would not fight against him any more. The Dutch queen left the Netherlands to go and live safely in London, and German soldiers arrived in Amsterdam.

People were filled with fear when they saw German soldiers everywhere on the streets of the city. At night, there were planes in the sky, and Anne often ran into her parents' room, terrified, when she heard them. But after a while, life began to continue almost like before. Children went back to school, their parents returned to work, and shops opened once more.

Nazi soldiers arriving in Amsterdam, 1940

Otto's businesses, Opekta and Pectacon, were now doing much better, and in December 1940, he moved his offices to a new building in the centre of Amsterdam, at 263 Prinsengracht. It was a tall building next to the canal, and at weekends, Anne liked to go there, often with her friend Hanneli Goslar, to use the typewriters and play with the telephones.

That winter, Hanneli had a new baby sister, so Anne was often at the Goslars' home, to play with the baby or take her out for a walk. Anne liked going to see films, too, and loved the exciting world of Hollywood: she cut pictures of famous actors out of magazines, and dreamed of becoming a film star herself. She had begun ice-skating, and in January 1941, she wrote to her cousin Bernd and the rest of her family in Switzerland, and told them that she was taking lessons and could now dance and jump on the ice.

In the first few months after the Nazis invaded the Netherlands, life did not change much for Jewish people. But from late 1940, notices that said 'Forbidden for Jews' started to appear

A typewri

263 Prinsengracht, Amsterdam

A 'Forbidden for Jews' notice, the Netherlands, 1940

all over Amsterdam. Soon, Jewish people could not go into cinemas, and had to stop doing important jobs, like directing businesses or working as doctors or dentists.

Edith Frank's brothers had already lost their family business, and Otto did not want the same thing to happen to him, so he closed Pectacon and opened a new company called Gies and Co. He was not the director of this company – in all the Gies and Co. papers, the director was Victor Kugler, who worked with Otto and who was not Jewish. But secretly, Otto continued to control Gies and Co. He did the same thing with Opekta, and made his friend Mr Kleiman the 'director'. In this way, Otto saved his businesses, and – unlike many other Jewish people in Amsterdam at that time – he was able to go on making a little money, too.

Summer 1941 was not a lot of fun for Anne and her friends. By that time, Jewish people were forbidden to go to beaches, swimming pools, parks, and hotels, and by September, almost all places – libraries, theatres, coffee shops, and restaurants – were closed to them. Jewish people could not own bicycles; and between eight o'clock in the evening and six in the morning, they were forbidden to go outside, even in their own gardens. It was difficult for children like Anne. But perhaps she had learned from her father to try and stay cheerful. It was too bad that they could not go to their favourite places any more, she wrote to her family in Switzerland, but there was nothing that they could do about it.

Otto and Anne Frank going to Miep and Jan's wedding, 16th July 1941

For one day in that summer of 1941, Anne and her family were able to forget their worries. On 16th July, Otto's secretary Miep married her boyfriend Jan Gies. Anne, Margot, Otto, and Edith all went to the wedding, and it was a happy day for everyone.

But on 8th August, more bad news arrived for Jewish families in the Netherlands. Jewish children now needed to go to special 'Jewish-only' schools, so Anne and Margot both had to leave the schools where they had been so happy. More than half of the children in Anne's class were Jewish, and they all had to move to a different school. Anne had to say goodbye to her dear teacher Mrs Kuperus, and to many of her friends – and she cried on her last day in her old class.

Anne started at her new Jewish school in October 1941. She only knew one person there – her friend Hanneli Goslar – and they were in different classes at first, so Anne felt lonely and afraid. But in fact, the next few months at the new school went well. Anne still saw her friend Sanne, who was now at a different school, and she made a new friend too, called Jacqueline van Maarsen.

Anne at school, 1941

Jacqueline (or Jacque, the name everybody used for her) lived near Anne's home. Her mother was French, and she had dark hair and big blue eyes. She and Anne liked the same books, and Jacque, like Anne, loved films. Anne could talk to Jacque about everything, and although Anne's house was not far from Jacque's, they often stayed the night with each other.

At the beginning of 1942, there was sadness for Anne's family when Oma Hollander died. She had lived with them for nearly two years, and had always been there to listen to Anne when she wanted to talk, so Anne missed her grandmother very much.

Life was difficult for the Franks in many ways at that time, but they still tried to enjoy themselves as much as they could. They had a cat now, called Moortje, which Anne loved dearly. And although they could not go to the cinema any more, Anne and Jacque enjoyed going to the two ice cream shops that Jewish people could still visit. They had 'film nights' at the Franks' apartment, too: the girls made tickets and all their friends came to watch films on the Franks' projector – a kind of machine for showing films that people used at that time.

A projector

Otto and Edith found other ways to keep their daughters busy, too. They and their friends invited people who could play instruments to their houses and had small music evenings. Anne, Margot, and their friends also acted in children's plays at the Franks' apartment.

The Franks and their friends needed evenings like these to stop them thinking about their troubles. From the end of April 1942, Jewish people in the Netherlands were ordered to wear, at all times, yellow stars with the Dutch word *Jood* ('Jew') on them in black letters. Some non-Jewish people started wearing the stars themselves, because they wanted their neighbours to know that they did not like what the Nazis were doing. But there were some people in the Netherlands who had welcomed the Nazis, and who agreed with Hitler's ideas. There were more and more reports at that time of attacks on Jewish homes and businesses, and on Jewish people, too.

Jewish children and adults wearing yellow stars

Earlier that year, fifteen of the most important Nazi officers and men in Hitler's government had met near Berlin. There, they had discussed the 'final solution' – ideas which they thought were the answer to the 'problem' of Jewish people, and others who they did not like. By spring 1942, many people knew that the Nazis had decided to send all Jewish people away from the Netherlands, to concentration camps in Germany and Eastern Europe.

Otto had begun back in 1938 to try to find a safer country as a home for his family, although he and Edith had said nothing about this to Anne and Margot. But it was now very hard to find a new place to live. Otto decided to try to move his family from the Netherlands to the US, where Anne's uncles Walter and Julius lived. They did everything that they could to help, but Otto and his family needed the right papers and a lot of money. All through 1941, Otto wrote to an old friend who lived in the US asking for his help, but in December that year, when the papers and money were nearly ready for the Franks, the US entered the war against Germany. When that happened, the US stopped giving papers for travel from countries that were controlled by the Nazis. There was now no escape for the Frank family.

Otto Frank tried to stay cheerful. He heard on British radio that British and French soldiers would soon arrive near the Netherlands. And at night, he and his family listened to the planes on their way to attack German cities. They were the planes of the Allies (Britain, the US, France, and other countries which were now fighting together against Nazi Germany). With the help of the US, the Allies would soon win the war, Otto told his friend Hans Goslar, Hanneli's father.

5 Into hiding, July 1942

Sunday 5ᵗʰ July 1942 was a hot day in Amsterdam, and Anne Frank spent the afternoon reading at home. She had had a worrying conversation with her father a few days earlier. He had told her that she and her family would perhaps need to go into hiding: they would need to move to a special place where no one could find them. Otto, Edith, and their friends had heard that the Nazis wanted to move all Jewish people out of the Netherlands very soon. It had become very clear to Otto that his family were not at all safe.

But on that day in July, Anne was thinking about lots of other things. She had celebrated her thirteenth birthday a few weeks earlier, with a big group of friends and a film on the projector at home. Her favourite present had been her new diary, and that week she had written in it about her new boyfriend, Hello Silberberg. He was sixteen years old, and she knew that he was in love with her. He had been to visit her that morning, and he had promised to come back later.

As Anne sat reading, Margot came in to see her. Anne looked up lazily from her book, but she knew at once from the look on Margot's face that something was wrong. A letter had come, Margot said, and it told their father that he needed to go to a camp.

In fact, the order had come not for Otto Frank but for Margot herself – but Edith Frank, who opened the letter, had not wanted to tell that to her sixteen-year-old daughter. Four thousand letters like the one for Margot arrived at Jewish homes in the Netherlands that day, and they were mostly for fifteen- and sixteen-year-old boys and girls. The letters said that these young people should be ready to leave between 14th and 17th July. They also told them what to bring with them: two blankets; food for three days; a plate, cup, and spoon; a washbag; and two changes of clothes.

The next few hours were frightening and hard for Anne and her family. Otto was not at home that afternoon, because he had gone to visit friends, but when he arrived home and heard the news, he was calm. He said that they would go into hiding the next morning. And he told Anne and Margot to pack a small bag each before they went to bed that night.

Otto and Edith Frank had decided weeks before to go into hiding, but they had hoped to wait until the middle of July, because they were still getting their hiding place ready. Now their plan needed to happen at once.

At the back of the building on Prinsengracht where Otto worked, above the office kitchen, there was an 'annexe': some extra rooms which were joined to the offices of Otto's companies. Because there were many rooms in the front building, where the offices and warehouse were, no one who visited knew that there were more rooms at the back.

Otto had thought that this annexe would make a good hiding place both for his family and the family of Hermann van Pels, who he worked with. But first, he had needed to speak to the other people from his offices, who were not Jewish. Mr Kugler, Mr Kleiman, Bep, and Miep all worked for Gies and Co. and Opekta, and they were friends of the Franks. Otto needed their help, and he needed them to keep his secret. He knew that this was dangerous for them: anyone who helped Jewish people was sent to prison or killed if the Nazis heard about it. But when Otto had asked his friends for their help, they had agreed at once.

A Dutch resistance poster

There were many other non-Jewish people in the Netherlands at that time who helped to hide their Jewish friends and neighbours, and many who knew about people who were in hiding, but said nothing. A lot of people also joined the Resistance – a group which worked secretly against the Nazis. These people all knew how dangerous it was for them to stand in the way of Hitler's plans.

In the weeks before 5th July, Otto and Edith and the van Pelses had cleaned and emptied the annexe and then begun to move food, bedsheets, and kitchen things there. They had brought schoolbooks for their children, too: they did not want them to fall behind in their lessons while they were in hiding. Mr Kleiman's brother, who had a cleaning business, had secretly taken big pieces of furniture from the Franks' house to Mr Kleiman's apartment and then, when the offices were closed in the evenings or at weekends, to the annexe.

So, although the Franks now needed to go into hiding earlier than they had planned, the annexe was nearly ready. On the afternoon of 5th July, Otto and Edith told Miep and Jan Gies what had happened, and that evening, when it was dark, Miep and Jan arrived at the Franks' house to take shoes, books, and clothes away for them in their bags and pockets.

Anne and Margot were told that they would carry only their schoolbags when they left the house the next morning, so they needed to decide what to pack inside them. Anne put old letters and a few schoolbooks, and of course her diary, into her bag. She wanted to take things that made her think of the people and places that she loved. While she and Margot packed, Otto wrote a letter to his family in Switzerland. He could not tell them openly that he, Edith, Anne, and Margot were going into hiding, but his words made it clear.

The next morning, Anne's mother woke her up at five thirty. Anne dressed in as many clothes as possible, wearing a skirt over a dress, and several pairs of underclothes. She and her family could not carry suitcases, because they did not want anyone to know that they were going into hiding.

It was raining when Anne said goodbye to her cat Moortje and left home with her parents. Margot had gone already with Miep; and Anne, Otto, and Edith now walked along the wide, modern streets of South Amsterdam and on towards the centre of the city.

The secret annexe was on two floors at the back of the building on Prinsengracht, with an attic above. On one floor, there was a small bedroom for Otto and Edith Frank, a bathroom, a toilet, and an even smaller bedroom for Anne and Margot. On the floor above, there was a bigger room – a bedroom for Mr and Mrs van Pels by night, and the kitchen and sitting room for both families by day. Next to that, there was a very small room for the van Pelses' son, Peter, and above it, the attic.

When Anne and her parents arrived in the annexe, on 6th July 1942, the rooms were full of boxes, bedsheets, and all the things that the Franks and van Pelses had sent there in the weeks before, with the help of their friends from the offices. Edith and Margot were too tired and frightened to do anything, and they fell onto their beds, unable to move. But for the rest of that day, and the day after, Anne and her father unpacked the boxes, put things in cupboards, cleaned the floors, and made curtains from old clothes to cover the windows and keep the annexe secret from those who lived nearby.

Anne did not know how long she would be in the annexe, or when she would see her home or her friends again. But she was too busy, and too tired, to think about the great changes in her life, and the dangers for her family.

The annexe

Illustration by Chantal van Wessel and Frederik Ruys

1 The attic	**4** The bathroom
2 Peter van Pels's room	**5** Otto and Edith's room
3 Mr and Mrs van Pels's room, the kitchen, and the sitting room	**6** Anne and Margot's room

6   Life in the annexe

Mr and Mrs van Pels and their son Peter joined the Franks in the annexe a week later, on 13th July. At first, Anne was excited to have another family there. Hermann van Pels was a tall, large man, who had worked in the meat business before he joined Otto's company. His wife, Auguste, liked to wear nice clothes, and she made Anne laugh when she arrived in the annexe with a chamber pot – a pot to use at night as a toilet! Mr and Mrs van Pels's son Peter was nearly sixteen, and he was quiet and uncomfortable with other people. Anne did not think that she would enjoy spending time with him.

Hermann van Pels   Auguste van Pels   Peter van Pels

At that time, when the Franks and van Pelses had just arrived in the annexe, everyone still thought that the war would end soon. Both families hoped that they would only need to live there for a few weeks or months. But while they were there, it was very important that they lived secretly. They had to be very careful, and not let anyone see or hear them. They did not want to put their own lives, or the lives of the friends who were helping them, in danger.

Because of this, they quickly agreed how they should live. No one could leave the building at any time, and on weekdays, everyone had to be quiet during work hours. Although the people who worked in the offices – Mr Kleiman, Mr Kugler, Miep, and Bep – all knew about the annexe, there were workers in the warehouse during the day who did not. So any noise during work hours put the two families in danger of discovery.

Everyone had to get up by seven o'clock in the morning, and they each had a time when they could use the bathroom. After that, no one could use any water: the workers arrived in the warehouse at eight thirty, and the families did not want them to hear water in the pipes. Before eight thirty, the Franks and van Pelses also had to put everything away in the bedrooms, because by day these rooms became sitting rooms, kitchens, and studies. After that, Anne, Margot, and Peter did their schoolwork, with help from Otto; and while they worked, the adults read, made and fixed clothes or curtains, and quietly got food ready for lunch. After half past twelve, the people in the annexe could move around a bit more freely again. The warehouse workers went for lunch at that time, and after they had left, the people from the offices – the annexe's helpers – often came to visit.

Lunchtime visits from Bep, Miep, Mr Kugler, Mr Kleiman,

and Miep's husband Jan Gies were a great help to the two families in the annexe. These people from the outside world talked to Otto about work, brought news of the war, and listened to the worries and problems of both the adults and the children. Often they joined the two families for lunch in Mr and Mrs van Pels's room.

After lunch, everyone had to be quiet in the annexe once more. But at half past five, when Bep or Miep came to tell them that all the workers had gone home, they were free at last. Bep's father, who also knew that the families were in hiding, had built a big bookcase which covered the door to the annexe, to hide the entrance. In the evening, the door and the bookcase were opened, and everyone went out of the annexe and downstairs into the offices, where they listened to the news on Dutch or British radio.

The bookcase covering the annexe door
(Otto Frank, 1964)

Although Otto was not called a director of his companies any more, he controlled them secretly, and his friends and helpers, the 'directors', did not decide on anything until he had agreed to it. So in the evenings, he and Mr van Pels usually looked at what had happened in the offices that day. Peter van Pels liked to spend his evenings in the warehouse, and Anne and Margot sat in an office and worked at small jobs that Miep had left for them there.

There was only cold water in the annexe, so in the evening, when the Franks and van Pelses could get hot water from the office kitchen, they had baths. Each person took their turn to carry the big metal bath to a place in the office building where they could be alone, and then they filled it with hot water for a good wash.

Life in the annexe was desperately hard. The Franks and the van Pelses knew that they were luckier than many Jewish people, who were in concentration camps, or who were hiding in much smaller and less comfortable places. But their rooms were very small for two families, and because it was too dangerous to open any windows, it was much too hot in the summer. The people in the annexe only saw the outside world when they looked very carefully between the curtains in the front office at night, or when they went up to the attic. There, they could stand and look through the big window in the roof at the beautiful chestnut tree next to their building. For them, looking at the leaves on that tree was the only way to watch summer turn to autumn, or winter to spring.

The annexe's helpers did everything that they could to make life a little easier for the two families. Bep and Miep did all the shopping for the annexe, and brought food and other things that the families asked for. Every week, Mr Kugler came with newspapers and magazines, and he never forgot to buy Anne's favourite cinema and theatre magazine on a Monday. Miep brought books from the library every Saturday, and when someone had a birthday, or there was a special holiday, the helpers came with flowers and presents.

Shopping for seven people was not easy, but people in Amsterdam knew that a lot of Jewish people had gone into hiding, and many of them were happy to help and asked no questions. A friend of Mr Kleiman gave him bread for the families; meat came from someone who Mr van Pels knew; and Bep bought fruit for the families when it was cheap, and secretly took milk from the offices up to the annexe each day. Miep bought vegetables from a shop near the offices, and became friends with the owner. He soon guessed why she was there so often, but he never said a word to her about it.

In November 1942, another person joined the annexe. Fritz Pfeffer was Miep's dentist, and he had known the Frank family well, so when he asked Miep for her help to find a hiding place that winter, the families in the annexe said that he could join them.

Anne was excited at first when she heard that someone new was coming to live with them, but she soon became tired of Fritz Pfeffer. She had slept in a small room with her sister for the first few months in the annexe, but Margot now moved in with their parents, and Fritz took

Fritz Pfeffer

Margot's bed in the room with Anne. That was difficult for Anne, and for Fritz, too. They both wanted to be alone in the small room when they were writing, reading, or working, and they soon began to argue.

Fritz and Anne were not the only ones who argued a lot in the annexe. Anne had never really seen her parents argue, and she was surprised by the big fights that Mr and Mrs van Pels often had. Her mother and Mrs van Pels also argued a lot about the children. The van Pelses thought that Anne talked too much, and that she needed to be more polite – and they told Otto and Edith again and again that they were too soft on their younger daughter.

As time went on, the two families argued more and more about food. Because of the war, it was difficult for the annexe helpers to find good food, and things like fruit became very expensive. Often the people in the annexe (like the Dutch people in the city around them) had to eat the same vegetables, which were old and bad, every day for weeks.

Money was difficult, too. The people in the annexe used money that they had saved to pay for food and other things that they needed, and Otto got some money from his businesses. But after a time, things got harder and harder, and the Franks and van Pelses had to sell jewellery and other valuable things that they had brought with them, to pay for what they needed.

The van Pelses, the Franks, and Fritz Pfeffer soon knew everything about each other, and the conversation at mealtimes was sometimes very difficult. Books and studying helped them all to survive. Anne loved history, and read everything that Miep and Mr Kleiman could get for her, and she enjoyed learning about Europe's kings and queens. Margot and Peter worked hard at their studies, too, and some of the adults learned languages. They wanted to be busy, but they were also thinking about the future, and about where they wanted to live after the war.

7   Hopes and fears, 1942–1944

All through her first year in the secret annexe, Anne's diary was very important to her. It was the first thing that she had packed in her bag the night before the Franks went into hiding, and although she did not write in it often at first, from the end of September 1942, she wrote something almost every day.

Around that time, she decided to write her diary in letters to 'pretend friends' – friends who were not real people. She took their names from a Dutch book called *Joop ter Heul* that she had read before she went into hiding. Later, she chose just one of those names, and began every letter in her diary 'Dear Kitty'.

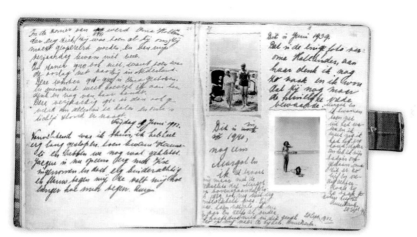

Anne's writing

Everyone in the annexe knew that Anne was writing a diary, and she sometimes read pages of it aloud to make people laugh. In her diaries, Anne did not use the real names of the van Pelses and of Fritz Pfeffer – she called the van Pelses the van Daans, and gave Fritz Pfeffer the name Albert Dussel. By the end of 1942, she had filled the red, white, and green notebook that her father had given her, so the annexe helpers brought her office books and pieces of paper to write on.

Anne's diaries clearly show the hopes, dreams, fears, and troubles of a young girl in an extraordinary time and place. In her teenage years, at an age when many young girls and boys begin to break away from their families a little, Anne had to be with hers, in a few very small rooms, all day and every day. She had no friends to talk to, and she could not escape somewhere when she wanted to be alone.

In her diaries, Anne spoke often of the problems that she had with her mother. Anne and Edith Frank were very different, and in Anne's eyes, Edith could not do anything right. Anne still loved her father – her dear Pim – very much, she wrote. But as time went on, she said often in her diaries that neither of her parents understood how much older she now felt.

When Bep or Miep or one of the other helpers came into the annexe, with the wind in their clothes and the cold on their faces, Anne desperately wanted to go outside. Often, she went up to the attic to look at the beautiful chestnut tree and to watch the birds in the sky, and although it made her feel better to see these things, she missed the world outside terribly. In December 1943, she wrote in her diary about this. She wanted to ride a bicycle or dance, she wrote – to feel young, and to know that she was free.

Just before she had gone into hiding, Anne had begun to have boyfriends, and when she arrived in the annexe, she thought often of some of the boys who she had known in Amsterdam. She thought about Hello Silberberg, who she had seen on that last day before the Franks left their home. Now there was only one boy who she could talk to – Peter van Pels. She had not been interested in him at first, and had thought that he was boring, but by early 1944, she began to notice when he was looking at her.

Soon Anne and Peter were spending hours together, and talking about their problems, and their hopes and fears for the future. Anne waited for her first kiss from Peter, and for a while, she wanted only to be with him. But as time passed, she began to lose interest in him. He did not think about things as deeply as she did, she wrote in her diary.

By spring 1944, Anne was beginning to change in other ways, too. She knew that she wanted more from the world than her mother and Mrs van Pels: she did not want to be a housewife like them. She wanted to do something with her life, she wrote in her diary in April 1944. She wanted to be useful, or to make people happy.

Anne was thinking a lot at that time about her love of writing. Her diaries were still very important to her, but she had begun to write short stories, too – some about life in the annexe, and others that were for children. She wanted to be a writer, she now said, because writing made her feel so much better about her worries.

On the radio in March 1944, someone from the Dutch government asked people to keep their wartime diaries and letters. He said that the government wanted to bring these papers together after the war to show everyone how difficult people's lives had been. Anne continued to write her diary every day, but she now looked back at her old diaries, too, cutting from them and writing parts again. She wanted to put her diaries together into a book which she decided to call *Het Achterhuis* ('The House Behind').

But while Anne still had dreams for the future, her days were full of very real fears, too. A lot of Jewish people had lived near the annexe when the Franks first arrived, and from the attic window, she had watched when many of them were taken away by the Gestapo (the Nazi secret police). She had seen these Nazis hit the adults with sticks while their children cried. Because Anne listened to Dutch radio with her family every night, she knew that these people were first taken to a big camp in the Netherlands called Westerbork, and then to the concentration camps in Poland, where most of them died.

Nazis taking Jewish people from Amsterdam, 1943

Often Anne lay awake at night, listening to every noise. Like the others in the annexe, she was afraid. She knew that by then, many people in Amsterdam were desperate for food and money – and the Nazis paid well for any news of Jewish people in hiding. Had somebody found out about them, and told the Gestapo about their secret hiding place? Were the Nazis coming to take them away?

There were several burglaries in the office warehouse while the two families and Fritz Pfeffer were living in the annexe, and after one of these, they lay terrified in the dark while the Gestapo looked around the building. At one moment, they heard someone come right up to the bookcase that covered the door to the annexe.

When planes flew above, and bombs fell on the streets of Amsterdam, Anne and all the others in the annexe were afraid of burning to death in their hiding place. There was the problem of illness, too. Anne had become very ill with a fever in winter 1943. She had got better in the end, but her family could not call a doctor, so they had had to wait and hope, without any help.

Planes dropping bombs on Amsterdam

On 27th November 1943, Anne wrote in her diary about a dream that she had about her friend Hanneli. In the dream, Hanneli was wearing dirty old clothes, and her face was thin and sad. She was crying, and she asked Anne to help her. Anne probably knew by that time that the Gestapo had arrested Hanneli and her family in June 1943 and sent them to concentration camps.

But in June 1944, there was at last some good news from the outside world. The Allies had invaded France, which the Nazis had controlled since 1940, so in the annexe, everyone was excited. They hoped that the Allies would now free Europe from the Nazis. Perhaps Anne would be back at school before too long.

Newspapers reporting the Allies' invasion of France, June 1944

8   Arrest, August 1944

It is 4th August 1944 – and a beautiful sunny day. Otto Frank is at the top of the annexe, in Peter's room, helping him with his homework, when he hears a noise. He recognizes every sound in these rooms where he has lived for two years, so he knows at once that something is not right. But he has been ready for this moment, and feared it. The door opens suddenly, and a man with a gun walks in. He shouts at Otto and Peter, and pushes them into the next room, where another man is watching Mr and Mrs van Pels. They are waiting in silence, terrified, with their hands above their heads.

Shaking, Otto and the van Pelses follow these men downstairs. There are more men there, but only one – Karl Josef Silberbauer – is wearing the uniform of the Gestapo. The others are Dutch Nazis. Margot is crying, but Anne, Edith, Otto, Fritz, and the van Pelses wait quietly while the men question them.

Silberbauer asks Otto for any valuables, so Otto gives him the box where they keep their money and a few pieces of jewellery. Then Silberbauer sees Otto's office bag, and empties it out. He is looking for more money, but only papers, office books, and a red, white, and green notebook – Anne's diaries – fall to the floor.

Everyone has five minutes, Silberbauer tells them, to pack a small bag. When he speaks to Otto and hears that Otto fought for the German army in the First World War, he softens a little and gives them more time. They only have a few things to choose from, but their lives are in danger, and they are too terrified to think carefully.

Downstairs in the offices, another man is questioning Mr Kleiman and Mr Kugler. When they arrived at the building, the Nazis told Mr Kugler that they knew everything. Jews were hiding in the building, they said, and he needed to show them where they were. Mr Kugler had taken them around the building. There was nothing to see, he tried to show them. But the Nazis knew where to look for hiding places. They shook the bookcase when they came to it, and soon discovered the door behind it.

The Franks, the van Pelses, and Fritz Pfeffer are told to go outside, and because Mr Kugler and Mr Kleiman do not answer their questions, the Gestapo take them, too. The people from the annexe step outside for the first time in two years. Anne has waited all those months to feel the air on her face, but this is not what it was like in her dreams. She is not a free young woman, but a prisoner of the Nazis.

* * *

Silberbauer and his men took their prisoners to the Gestapo office in southern Amsterdam, where they were locked in prison rooms for the night. Then, the next day, the people from the annexe were taken to a different prison near the centre of Amsterdam. They knew what was waiting for them. After two years as prisoners in the annexe, they were now going to a concentration camp.

Mr Kugler and Mr Kleiman were taken to a different prison. Before they went, Otto had a moment to speak to Mr Kleiman. He felt terrible, he said, that Mr Kleiman was now in danger because he had helped his Jewish friends. But Mr Kleiman was not sorry. He had wanted to do it, he said, and he was pleased that he had.

After the war, in 1948, the Dutch police tried to find out

who had told the Nazis about the families in the annexe at 263 Prinsengracht. Over the years, many people have asked the same question – but we will probably never know the answer. Did one of the people who came to the warehouse during the years 1942–1944 see or hear something, and tell the Gestapo? Did one of the neighbours see a light between the curtains of the annexe one night? Or were the Gestapo looking for something different, and did chance bring them to the annexe that day?

Anne wrote in her diary for the last time on 1st August 1944. After the Gestapo left the building at 263 Prinsengracht, Bep and Miep went quietly up to the annexe. The police had pulled everything out of the cupboards. On the floor there were books and papers, and Anne's diaries. Bep and Miep did not stay long. It was too dangerous. But they took some library books, and the diaries, and put the diaries in Miep's desk in the offices.

Anne's diary, 1st August 1944

9

The camps, 1944–1945

By early August 1944, when the annexe was discovered, Hitler's armies were in serious difficulty. The Allies had moved into France, and were liberating large parts of the country from the Germans. Hitler had invaded the Soviet Union (modern-day Russia and some of the countries around it) in 1941. But the Soviet Union had fought back, and Russian armies were now travelling through Poland, towards Germany.

So although the Franks, the van Pelses, and Fritz Pfeffer were frightened when they left Amsterdam, they were a little hopeful, too. Perhaps the end of the war would come soon and save them, they told themselves.

They were going first, by train, to Westerbork, the camp in the Netherlands where the Nazis sent Jewish people before they moved them to the concentration camps of Germany and Eastern Europe. When the train left Amsterdam, the doors were locked, but Anne and the others had food and were able to look out of a window, and Otto said later that they were almost cheerful as they travelled. Outside, it was summer, and Anne did not leave the window. After so long inside, it was exciting for them all to see fields and villages.

But when they arrived at Westerbork late that afternoon, they saw how bad things were. Because they had been in hiding, the group were punished, and given less food than the other prisoners in the camp. Their hair was cut very short, their clothes were taken from them, and they were given blue uniforms to wear.

Anne and the others were in Westerbork for nearly a month. Each day, from five o'clock in the morning, Anne and Margot had to work in a dirty building, cleaning old aeroplane parts. Lunch was watery soup and a piece of old bread. Otto lived in a different building from Edith and the girls, but he was able to visit them and he tried to keep them cheerful.

People who met Anne in Westerbork said that she was very friendly, and talked to the other prisoners a lot. Everyone there was afraid, of course, of the concentration camps. They knew now about the terrible things that happened there, and about the gas chambers – rooms that the Nazis filled with poisoned air, killing everyone inside. But while Anne and her family were together, and still in the Netherlands, they felt safe. Good news about the war reached them and kept them hopeful, too: on 25th August, Paris was liberated, and the Allies began to move towards Belgium and the Netherlands.

Jewish people in Westerbork camp

Every Tuesday, a train filled with prisoners left Westerbork to go to the concentration camps of Eastern Europe. The war was coming to an end, and the train that left Westerbork on 3rd September was the last one from the camp. The night before, the list of all the people travelling on that train was called out. The Franks, the van Pelses, and Fritz Pfeffer were all on the list.

The journey from Westerbork was very different to the one from Amsterdam. The train was crowded and cold, and there was no food, water, or toilet. It travelled east for three days, but because there were so many people in the train, no one could sleep – or even sit down. People were tired and desperate, and sometimes they argued and fought.

On the third night, the train arrived at the concentration camp at Auschwitz, in Poland. Under strong searchlights, the Nazi guards, with their big dogs, shouted that everyone should get out of the train. Then, anyone who was ill or old, and all children younger than fifteen, were taken from their loved ones and sent to the gas chambers, where they were killed at once.

The Franks' names on the Auschwitz list

Jewish people arriving at Auschwitz concentration camp, 1944

As people screamed and cried, Anne was taken to join another group of terrified people. She had turned fifteen a few months earlier, and she was now sent to the women's camp, together with Margot, Edith, and Mrs van Pels. Did Anne watch when her father was pushed away from them to go to the men's camp, with Fritz Pfeffer, Mr van Pels, and Peter? And did she know then that she would never see Otto – her dear Pim – again?

The women were taken to a building where their heads were shaved and they had to shower in ice-cold water. Then they were given dirty old grey clothes to wear, and their camp numbers were burned onto their arms. They had to sleep in a cold and dirty building that was full of hungry, desperate women.

And so life in Auschwitz began. Every morning at half past three, the women were called out from their building to eat a thin brown soup for breakfast. Then they had to stand in the big open square of the camp. They often had to wait there for hours while they were counted and while those who had done anything wrong – working too slowly,

for example, or going to the bathroom at the wrong time –
were punished. These poor prisoners were hit violently, or
sent to a room in a special part of the camp where there were
no windows and where they had to sleep on the floor.

Prisoners who were not strong enough to work were also in
danger. They were taken to the gas chambers because the Nazi
officers knew that they were not useful to them any more.

After this start to the day, the prisoners were then sent to
work, digging up grass, while the guards stood nearby and
shouted at them to work faster.

Auschwitz concentration camp

On 30th October, Anne and Margot were moved once more, this time to the Bergen-Belsen concentration camp in Germany. Edith was not moved with her daughters, and she could not survive without them. People who saw her in those last months said that she was very distressed, and stopped fighting to stay alive after Anne and Margot left. She died on 6th January 1945. She was forty-four years old.

There were no gas chambers at Bergen-Belsen, but life there was awful. There was almost no water or food, and many of the prisoners were ill.

But there was surprising news for Anne in February 1945. Mrs van Pels had joined Anne and Margot in Bergen-Belsen, and one day she met a girl from another part of the camp who was asking for Anne Frank. It was Hanneli Goslar. There were fences between the different parts of the camp, but Hanneli and Anne were able to see each other a few times. Hanneli got better food in her part of the camp, so twice she brought a small packet of food and threw it over the fence for Anne. The first time, another woman caught it, but the second packet reached her.

Hanneli's father died soon after that, so she did not go out to the fence for a while, and when she asked for Anne again, she heard that the Nazis had moved her to a different part of the camp.

As the winter went on, Anne and Margot became very ill with typhus. They were moved to a special building for very sick people, and there they quickly became worse. They both had terrible fevers, and were in great pain. Sometime between the end of February and the middle of March, Margot fell from her bed and died; and Anne died a few days later, alone. The war was nearly at an end, but they were not strong enough to fight for their lives any more.

Soldiers freeing prisoners at Bergen-Belsen, 1945

Only a few weeks later, on 15th April, British soldiers arrived to free the prisoners of Bergen-Belsen. When the British army arrived there, they could not believe what they found. The dead bodies of ten thousand people were lying where they had fallen on the ground. There were sixty thousand survivors in the camp, but because they were so ill and hungry, they continued to die in the months after the camp was liberated.

At the start of the war, there had been one hundred and forty thousand Jewish people living in the Netherlands. One hundred and seven thousand were taken by train to the concentration camps of Eastern Europe between 1941 and 1944. Only five thousand of them returned home alive.

A memorial to Margot and Anne, Bergen-Belsen

MARGOT FRANK 1926 – 1945 ANNE FRANK 1929 – 1945

10   The diaries

When Hanneli met Anne in Bergen-Belsen in February 1945, Anne told her that her parents, Edith and Otto, were both dead. Anne said that she did not want to live any more; she seemed 'broken' to Hanneli. She did not know that dear Pim, her father, was still alive.

Otto had stayed in Auschwitz after Anne and Margot were taken to Bergen-Belsen. The Nazis gave him hard, heavy work every day, and after several months, he became too ill to move. He was saved by a doctor who brought him into a building for prisoners who were sick. Otto did not become stronger there, but he did not have to work.

He was visited by Peter van Pels, who was working in the camp post office. Because of Peter's job in the camp, he got more food than the other prisoners, and he brought some to Otto every day. As the Russian armies came nearer and nearer in January 1945, the Germans moved many prisoners from Auschwitz to another camp at Mauthausen, and Peter wanted Otto to go there with him. But because Otto was not strong enough to move, he stayed at Auschwitz. Staying there saved his life. The Russians liberated Auschwitz on 27th January 1945: Otto was free, and alive.

Because it was the end of the war, and travel was so difficult, it took Otto four months to get back to the Netherlands. When he arrived in Amsterdam, on 3rd June 1945, he went to live with Miep and Jan Gies.

Otto knew already that Edith had died, but he hoped desperately to find Anne and Margot. He put notices in newspapers, and read every name on the lists of survivors that were sent from the camps. And he questioned everyone he met who had been a prisoner, when people began to return home. At last, in the middle of July, he spoke to two sisters who had known Anne and Margot in Bergen-Belsen, and who had tried to help them in their final days. They had terrible news for him. Otto now wrote to his mother and brothers to tell them that Anne and Margot were dead.

When Miep heard the news that she had feared so much, she took some papers and notebooks from her desk in the Prinsengracht offices and gave them to Otto. They were Anne's diaries, which she and Bep had found in the annexe on the terrible day of the arrests. She had kept them safe, and had hoped to return them to Anne one day. She had never read them. Now, she decided, they should go to Otto.

Otto could not read the diaries at first because he was too distressed. When at last he began to look at them, he translated small parts from Dutch into German and sent them to his mother, Omi Frank, in Basel, and to other people who had known Anne. He did not think of publishing the diaries at that time, but friends and family who read them

Anne's diaries

were deeply moved by Anne's words, and they told Otto that he should make the diaries into a book. That, of course, was what Anne had wanted.

So Otto began work on the diaries. He used some of the new pages that Anne had written after March 1944, and some of the pages from her first diaries. He took out a few parts because he did not think that they were interesting for other people, or because he did not want anyone outside his family to read them. When he had finished, he showed the book to close friends, and it was then given to a Dutch historian, who wrote about it for a newspaper. At once, people began to show an interest in Anne's diaries, and in June 1947, a small Dutch company called Contact published the book. It was called *Het Achterhuis* ('The House Behind'), the name that Anne had chosen.

The book sold quickly in the Netherlands, and in 1950, it was translated and sold in France and West Germany. But it did not become a bestseller until it was translated into English in 1952. In April 1944, in Anne's diary, she had said that she wanted to go on living after she died. Now she was famous around the world.

Translations of Anne's diaries

Otto began to get thousands of letters from young people who had read the book. He had married again in 1953, and he and his wife, who was also an Auschwitz survivor, spent several hours a day answering the letters. At the end of each letter, Otto always had an important message for the person who had written to him. He hoped, he told them, that because they had read Anne's book, they would always try to keep peace in the world, and to make it a place where anyone can live safely.

Because of the success of the book, a play about Anne's diaries was made. It was shown for the first time in New York in 1955. This was followed three years later by a film, *The Diary of Anne Frank*. Over the years, the diaries were published in seventy different languages, and more than thirty million books were sold.

Otto continued to work in the canalside building at 263 Prinsengracht where he and his family had hidden for two years. But in the 1950s, a company wanted to knock it down and build a factory in its place. A group of people in Amsterdam worked together to save the building, and at last, they succeeded. On 3rd May 1960, it opened as a museum, the Anne Frank House. More than a million people now visit every year.

Today, many streets, schools, and other buildings across the Netherlands carry the name Anne Frank, and there are memorials to her around the world. One of these is in the Anne Frank Memorial Park in the Jerusalem hills, in Israel. In this park, in 1960, Otto Frank planted the first of six million trees that now grow there. There is one tree for every Jewish person who died during the Holocaust – Hitler's terrible attack on Europe's Jews. Most of these people are not well known like Anne Frank, but each of them, like her, had a terrible and painful story.

In 1963, Otto Frank started the Anne Frank Foundation, and it is still working today. It brings together young men and women, boys and girls from around the world, to work for peace between different people and countries, and to keep alive the stories of Anne Frank and the other millions who were killed by Hitler's Nazis.

When he died in 1980, Otto Frank left Anne's diaries to the government of the Netherlands, and in 1986, they were published again, with new parts that only Otto had read before. The real diary and notebooks are now kept at the Anne Frank House.

Anne Frank House Museum, 263 Prinsengracht

11   Family and friends

Otto Frank was the only person from the annexe at Prinsengracht who survived until the end of the war. Hermann van Pels hurt his finger while he was working at Auschwitz in October 1944, so the Nazis sent him to the gas chambers. Fritz Pfeffer died in a camp in Germany in December 1944.

Peter van Pels died a few months after he left Auschwitz to go to Mauthausen concentration camp in January 1945. His mother, Auguste van Pels, probably died on the journey from Bergen-Belsen to a camp in Czechoslovakia, in April that year.

Many of Anne's friends died in the concentration camps, too. Susanne Ledermann ('Sanne') was sent to Auschwitz, like Anne, but she was killed in the gas chambers when she arrived there in November 1943. Hanneli Goslar lost both her parents, but survived. The Nazis put her and her sister on a train from Bergen-Belsen to Czechoslovakia, with other prisoners, in April 1945, but after they had travelled for nearly two weeks through Germany, the Russians found the train, and those who were still alive were freed. Hanneli was very ill, and had to stay in hospital for several months. While she was there, Otto began visiting her; and he cared for her and her sister like his own daughters when they returned to the Netherlands. Later, Hanneli and her sister went to live with a Dutch family in Basel, and Hanneli became a nurse.

The people who helped the Franks, the van Pelses, and Fritz Pfeffer while they were in hiding were all given awards after the war. Mr Kleiman and Mr Kugler had both returned from the concentration camps. Mr Kleiman was sent home in September 1944; and Mr Kugler escaped in March 1945 and went into hiding until the Netherlands was liberated. After the war, he moved to Canada.

Bep married and had four children – and continued to be a friend of Otto's to the end of his life. Miep Gies managed Otto's companies until Mr Kleiman returned in September 1944. She stopped working in 1947 to care for her husband Jan, and for Otto. In the 1980s, she worked with an American writer on a book called *Anne Frank Remembered*, and she died in 2010, seventeen years after Jan.

Anne's uncles Julius and Walter spent the rest of their lives in the US. They had directed the family business in Germany, but in the US, they worked in a factory and made just enough money to live. After they heard the terrible news about their sister, and about Anne and Margot, their lives were never the same again. They lived alone, unhappily. Julius died in 1967, and his brother soon after, in 1968.

Otto Frank had moved to Basel in the 1950s, and he was ninety-one years old when he died. He had spent most of his life after the war keeping Anne's story alive – and through it the painful stories of so many others, too.

Otto Frank , 1976

apartment *(n)* a group of rooms to live in, on one floor of a larger building

attack *(v & n)* to start fighting or hurting somebody or something

attic *(n)* the room under the roof of a house

award *(n)* something valuable or important, like money, etc. that you give to somebody who has done something special

believe *(v)* to feel sure that something is true

bookcase *(n)* a piece of furniture that you keep books in

burglary *(n)* the crime of going into a building to steal things

camp *(n)* a place where people stay for a short time, for example a prison camp or work camp

canal *(n)* a long, narrow piece of water made by people through land for boats

celebrate *(v)* to do something when you are happy for a special reason or because it is a special day

cheerful *(adj)* showing happiness

chestnut tree *(n)* a tree with large leaves that grows large, round, brown nuts

control *(v & n)* to decide how a country, a company, etc. works

cousin *(n)* the child of your aunt or uncle

curtain *(n)* something in front of a window which you can move to cover it or to make a room dark

dentist *(n)* a person who looks after your teeth for their job

desperate *(adj)* having no hope and ready to do anything to get what you want; **desperately** *(adv)*

direct *(v)* to manage or control somebody or something

distressed *(adj)* very unhappy or worried

economy *(n)* how a country spends its money and makes, buys, and sells things

educated *(adj)* A person who is educated has studied and learned a lot.

fence *(n)* a thing like a wall that is made of pieces of wood or metal

festival *(n)* a special time which people usually celebrate together

fever *(n)* If you have a fever, your body is too hot because you are ill.

forbidden *(adj)* If something is forbidden, you may not do it.

government *(n)* the group of people who control a country

guard *(n)* a person who stops somebody from escaping

history *(n)* the study of things that happened in the past;
   historian *(n)* a person who studies or writes about history

ice-skating *(n)* to move on ice in special boots that have long pieces of metal on the bottom

instrument *(n)* a thing that you use for playing music

invade *(v)* to go into another country to attack it

jam *(n)* sweet food made from fruit and sugar; you eat jam on bread

Jew *(n)* a person who follows the religion of Judaism;
   Jewish *(adj)*

jewellery *(n)* things like rings that people wear; they are often made of expensive metals or stones

kiss *(n)* touching somebody with your lips to show love

liberate *(v)* to make somebody or something free; **liberated** *(adj)*

list *(n)* a lot of names or other pieces of information that you write or say

memorial *(n)* a thing, place, or building that is made for remembering someone or something

play *(n)* a story that you watch in the theatre

poisoned *(adj)* when you add something to food, drink, or the air that will kill someone or make them very ill

political party *(n)* a group who have the same ideas; if people vote for them, they can control government

product *(n)* something that people make or grow to sell

publish *(v)* to make and sell a book, magazine, or newspaper

soup *(n)* hot food that you eat from a bowl; to make it, you cook things like vegetables or meat in water

spice *(n)* something made from a plant; you can put it in food to give it a stronger taste

survive *(v)*   to continue to live in or after a difficult or dangerous time; **survivor** *(n)*

synagogue *(n)*   a building where Jewish people meet

teenager *(n)*   a person who is between thirteen and nineteen years old

terrified *(adj)*   very afraid

translate *(v)*   to change what somebody has said or written in one language to another language

typhus *(n)*   a serious disease which gives people fevers and pain, and often ends in death

vote *(v)*   to draw an 'X' on a piece of paper to help choose the political party that controls a country; **voter** *(n)*

war *(n)*   fighting between countries or between groups of people

warehouse *(n)*   a big building where people keep things before they sell them

Anne Frank's family tree

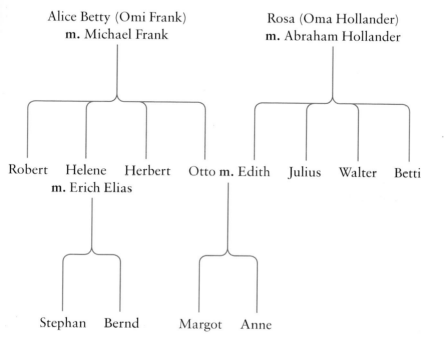

Alice Betty (Omi Frank)
m. Michael Frank

Rosa (Oma Hollander)
m. Abraham Hollander

Robert   Helene   Herbert   Otto **m.** Edith   Julius   Walter   Betti
m. Erich Elias

Stephan   Bernd   Margot   Anne

About this family tree

- 'm.' means 'married to'
- Anne and her sister Margot called their grandmothers Omi Frank and Oma Hollander; 'Omi' and 'Oma' mean 'Grandma' (a short word for 'Grandmother')

Timeline

1929	• 12ᵗʰ **June** Anne Frank is born in Frankfurt, Germany • **October** World economy crashes
1933	• **January** Hitler becomes Chancellor of Germany
1934	• **February** Anne joins her family in Amsterdam
1938	• **March** Hitler's Nazis invade Austria • **November** Anne's uncles, Julius and Walter Hollander, are taken to concentration camps
1939	• **March** Hitler's Nazis invade Czechoslovakia • **September** Hitler's Nazis invade Poland; France and Britain go to war against Germany
1940	• **May** Hitler's Nazis invade the Netherlands, and Belgium and France • **June** Italy enters the war, fighting with Germany • **December** Otto Frank moves his businesses to new offices at 263 Prinsengracht, in Amsterdam
1941	• **June** Hitler's Nazis invade the Soviet Union • **October** Anne has to move to a new Jewish school • **December** Japan attacks Pearl Harbour, and the US goes to war against Germany, Italy, and Japan
1942	• **June** Anne starts to write her diary • **July** Anne and her family go into hiding with the van Pels family • **November** Fritz Pfeffer also moves into the secret annexe
1944	• **June** The D-Day landings – the Allies' armies arrive on the beaches of Normandy (France) and invade France • **August** The annexe is discovered by the Nazis • **August** The Allies reach Paris and the city is liberated • **September** Anne and her family, the van Pels family, and Fritz Pfeffer are taken to Auschwitz concentration camp • **October** Anne and Margot are moved to Bergen-Belsen concentration camp
1945	• **January** Edith Frank dies in Auschwitz concentration camp • **January** Auschwitz concentration camp is liberated by the Russian army • **March** Anne and Margot die in Bergen-Belsen concentration camp • **April** Bergen-Belsen concentration camp is liberated by the British army • **May** End of the war in Europe • **June** Otto Frank returns to Amsterdam • **August** The US drops the first atomic bombs on Japan • **September** Second World War ends
1947	• **June** Anne's diaries are published as *Het Achterhuis*, or 'The House Behind'
1960	• **May** The Anne Frank House opens
1963	• **January** Anne Frank Foundation starts
1980	• **August** Otto Frank dies

The Holocaust

The Holocaust was when Hitler's Nazis killed around six million Jews during the Second World War. Around five million people from other groups were also killed. The Holocaust happened in Germany, in the countries which Nazi Germany invaded, and in the countries that fought together with Germany. It started when Hitler became the Chancellor of Germany, and finished when the war in Europe came to an end in the summer of 1945. Because of the Holocaust, the Frank family left Germany in 1933 and went into hiding in Amsterdam.

So how did the Holocaust happen? In Germany in the 1920s, like in many other countries in the world, life was hard. Hitler wanted to control the country through his Nazi party. He told people that the economy had crashed because of the Jews. They were the reason why people did not have jobs, Hitler said. These lies about the Jews made a lot of people hate them. From 1933, when Hitler became the Chancellor of Germany, the Nazis started to build concentration camps, and life became more and more difficult and dangerous for Jewish people. Then, from 1941, the Nazis started to kill Jewish people.

Anne's diaries are special because other teenagers who lived and died during the Holocaust cannot tell us the story of what happened to them. Many people also hope that because of books like Anne's diaries, nobody will forget the Holocaust and the people who died.

Think ahead

1 **Look at the front and back cover. What are you going to read about in this book? Tick (✓) five things.**

a family who hide   ☐
famous diaries   ☐
a terrible time in European history   ☐
a war   ☐
an old man   ☐
a young girl   ☐

2 **What do you know about Anne Frank? Choose the correct words to complete the sentences.**

1 Anne Frank *was / was not* born in Germany.
2 She started writing a diary when she was *10 / 13*.
3 Her book is about things that *really happened / didn't really happen*.
4 Anne *had / did not have* an easy life.

3 **RESEARCH** **Find out the answer to these questions about Anne Frank.**

1 Can you read Anne Frank's book in your language?
2 If your answer to question 1 is 'Yes', what is the book's title in your language?

Chapter check

CHAPTER 1 Correct the underlined words.

1 In June 1942, Europe was at <u>peace</u>.
2 On her thirteenth birthday, Anne was in <u>Germany</u>.
3 Anne's presents were on the table in the <u>bedroom</u>.
4 The birthday present that Anne wanted most of all was a <u>game</u>.

CHAPTER 2 Are these sentences true or false?

1 Margot was louder than Anne.
2 Otto spent a lot of time playing with his children.
3 Anne's parents were from German Jewish families.
4 In the early 1930s, Hitler's Nazi party became less important.
5 The Nazis made life more difficult and dangerous for Jewish people in Germany.
6 In 1933, the Franks made plans to stay in Frankfurt.

CHAPTER 3 Match.

1 Oma Hollander   a Otto's secretary
2 Hanneli Goslar   b Otto's business partner
3 Johannes Kleiman   c Peter's mother
4 Auguste van Pels   d Anne's school friend
5 Miep Santrouschitz   e Edith's mother

CHAPTER 4 Number the sentences in the correct order, 1–5.

a Anne and Margot had to go to 'Jewish-only' schools.

b Anne's grandmother, Oma Hollander, died.

c Otto Frank moved his businesses to a new building.

d Jewish people in the Netherlands had to start wearing yellow stars.

e Hitler's Nazis invaded the Netherlands.

CHAPTER 5 Complete the sentences with the correct words.

annexe   boxes   hiding   secret   schoolbag

1 The Franks needed to go into _____ to keep safe.

2 The building where Otto worked had an _____.

3 Otto needed his workers to keep a _____.

4 When Anne left home, she carried only her _____.

5 Anne worked hard with her father, unpacking

    _____.

CHAPTER 6 Match the sentence halves.

1 The two families agreed how to live…

2 A dentist called Fritz Pfeffer came…

3 The families sold jewellery…

4 Books and studying helped the families…

a to live in the annexe in November.

b to buy food and other things that they needed.

c to survive and keep busy.

d to keep the annexe secret.

CHAPTER 7 Tick (✓) the two sentences which are true.

1 ☐ At first when Anne lived in the annexe, she wrote in her diary every day.
2 ☐ In her diary, Anne wrote about her hopes and fears, and also about her problems.
3 ☐ Anne didn't know what was happening to Jewish people in the world outside the annexe.
4 ☐ Anne was frightened because of the burglaries in the offices and bombs that fell on Amsterdam's streets.

CHAPTER 8 Choose the correct answers.

1 When were Anne and the people in the annexe arrested?
  a ☐ 1st August 1944
  b ☐ 2nd August 1944
  c ☐ 4th August 1944

2 Who told the Gestapo about the secret annexe?
  a ☐ the neighbours
  b ☐ the warehouse workers
  c ☐ nobody knows

3 When did Anne write in her diary for the last time ?
  a ☐ 1st August 1944
  b ☐ 3rd August 1944
  c ☐ 4th August 1944

4 What things did Bep and Miep secretly take from the annexe after the arrest?
  a ☐ family photos
  b ☐ Anne's diaries
  c ☐ clothes

CHAPTER 9 Number the places where Anne went in the correct order, 1–3. Who was with Anne in each place?

Edith   Fritz Pfeffer   Hanneli Goslar   Margot
Mr van Pels   Mrs van Pels   Otto   Peter

a   Bergen-Belsen
b   Westerbork
c   A women's camp at Auschwitz

CHAPTER 10 Correct the <u>underlined</u> words.

1   After Auschwitz was liberated, Otto took four <u>weeks</u> to travel back to the Netherlands.
2   Miep gave Anne's <u>schoolbag</u> to Otto.
3   When Anne's diaries were translated into <u>French</u>, her name became known around the world.

CHAPTER 11 Complete the sentences with the correct people.

Anne's uncles   Hanneli   Miep   Otto

1   _____ was very ill when she was freed, but got better and became a nurse.
2   _____ helped write a book called *Anne Frank Remembered*.
3   _____ lived in the US, where they heard the terrible news about Edith, Anne, and Margot.
4   _____ worked hard to keep the Jewish people's story alive through Anne's diaries.

Focus on vocabulary

1 Complete the sentences with the correct words.

cheerful   guards   invaded   terrified

1 Anne and everyone in the annexe were _____ when there were burglaries in the warehouse.
2 Otto Frank tried hard to stay _____.
3 Germany _____ the Netherlands in May 1940.
4 There were many _____ in the camps to stop people escaping.

2 Write the words.

Across

1 to continue to live
3 to make someone's writing into a book
4 like a river, but built by people
6 someone aged thirteen to nineteen

Down

1 a hot food that people eat from bowls
2 someone who reads a lot and studies is like this
5 when countries fight each other

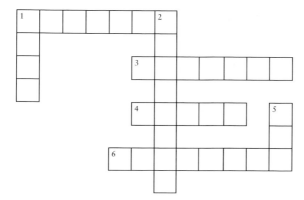

Focus on language

1 **Complete the sentences using *was* or *were* and the correct verbs.**

arrested ~~*kept*~~ *moved* *planted* *told*

   Anne's story __*was kept*__ alive by her diary.
1 Anne _____ that she could carry only her schoolbag.
2 Anne watched when neighbours _____ by the Gestapo.
3 Sick people _____ to a special building.
4 The first tree in the Anne Frank Memorial Park _____ by Otto Frank.

2 **DECODE** **Read the text and <u>underline</u> *who*. Then tick (✓) the correct sentences.**

For Anne and Margot, who both had new friends, and who quickly began to learn Dutch, life in Amsterdam was happy and fun. Their friends loved visiting their home. Mrs Frank liked to put special food on the table for her daughters' friends – and everybody loved Mr Frank, who always seemed cheerful.

1 a ☐ Anne had new friends, and Margot quickly began to learn Dutch.
   b ☐ Anne and Margot had new friends, and they quickly began to learn Dutch.
2 a ☐ Mr Frank always seemed cheerful.
   b ☐ Everybody always seemed cheerful.

Discussion

1 Read the dialogue. Why does each person think Anne's diaries are most important? <u>Underline</u> the two questions.

A: I think Anne's diaries are important because they made her life better.

B: What do you mean?

A: Well, they helped her to be busy. And they stopped her arguing too much while she was in hiding. What do you think?

B: I think Anne's diaries are important because they help make the world a place where anyone can live safely. I think they help people remember the Holocaust and the people who died.

A: That's true.

B: I think that people who read the diaries will help keep peace in the world, too.

2 What is your opinion? Tick (✓) the reason you think is most important. Discuss your answer with a partner. Use the questions from exercise 1.

I think Anne's diaries are important because...

☐ they helped her to be busy while she was in hiding.

☐ people everywhere know her name and remember her.

☐ they stop people forgetting the Holocaust.

☐ they stopped her arguing too much when she was in hiding.

☐ they helped her to be honest about how she felt.

☐ they help keep peace in the world.

☐ they gave her the chance to be a writer.

1 Think of books about people's lives during war (the books can be in English or your first language).

2 Read this summary of a book by someone who lived during the Second World War.

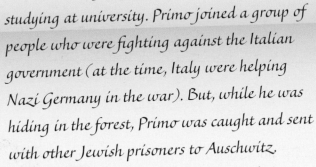

Primo Levi's book is called
<u>Survival in Auschwitz</u>. The
book is about the writer's
life during the Second
World War. At the start of
the book, Primo Levi was
a young Jewish-Italian
man who had just finished
studying at university. Primo joined a group of
people who were fighting against the Italian
government (at the time, Italy were helping
Nazi Germany in the war). But, while he was
hiding in the forest, Primo was caught and sent
with other Jewish prisoners to Auschwitz.

When Primo arrived at Auschwitz, his
life was very difficult. There was not enough
food and Primo had to work until he almost
died. He was helped by a man called Lorenzo

Perrone, who gave him some soup every day. Later, he was given a job that was more comfortable than his other work because he could be indoors during the winter. Doing this work, Primo was also able to steal things and use them to buy more food. Primo was at Auschwitz until the camp was liberated by the Russian army on 27th January 1945. After eleven months at Auschwitz, when many of the people around him had died, Primo had survived.

3 **Read the profile again and answer the questions.**

1 What was the name of the writer and the book?
2 What did the person in the book do before the war?
3 What happens to the person because of the war?
4 How does the book end?

4 CREATE Choose one of the books from exercise 1. For the book you choose, find the answers to the questions in exercise 3. Use the answers to write a summary.

5 COLLABORATE Share your summaries in small groups. Then, as a group, discuss why each book is important.

If you liked this Bookworm, why not try...

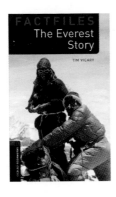

The Everest Story

STAGE 3

Tim Vicary

It is beautiful to look at, hard to reach, and terribly difficult to climb. Winds of 200 kilometres per hour or more scream across it day and night, while the temperature falls to -200°C or lower. Every year, some who try to climb the highest mountain in the world do not return.

But for a century, people have been coming to climb Everest – some alone, some in groups, but all with a dream of going to the highest place in the world. This is their story.

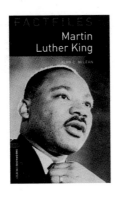

Martin Luther King

STAGE 3

Alan C. McLean

The United Stated in the 1950s and 60s was a troubled place. Black people were angry, because they did not have the same rights as whites. It was a time of angry words, or marches, of protests, a time of bombs and killings.

But above the angry noise came a voice of one man – a man of peace. 'I have a dream,' said Martin Luther King, and it was a dream of black people and white people living together in peace and freedom. This is the story of an extraordinary man, who changed America in his short life.